Rose of Thanks

Rose of Thanks

A BOOK OF INSPIRATION, PEACE AND JOY

Myrtle F. Jackson

ROSE OF THANKS
A BOOK OF INSPIRATION, PEACE AND JOY

iUniverse books may be ordered through booksellers or by contacting:

iUniverse
1663 Liberty Drive
Bloomington, IN 47403
www.iuniverse.com
1-800-Authors (1-800-288-4677)

ISBN: 978-1-4917-8651-2 (sc)
ISBN: 978-1-4917-8652-9 (e)

Library of Congress Control Number: 2015921124

Print information available on the last page.

iUniverse rev. date: 12/23/2015

For my sons,

Richard and Justin

Other books by Myrtle F. Jackson

God's Abounding Field
I Hear an Echo in the Wind

In Memory ...

Linda Marie Manor
1958–2005

The Rose

The rose is embraced
When its petals open wide.
A light from heaven transcends
The petals inside.
The rose is awesomely special
And uniquely ranked
In God's beautiful universe
We lift the rose of thanks!

—Myrtle F. Jackson

CONTENTS

INTRODUCTION

Every time I think about how great God is, I feel inspired to meditate more, pray more and live life to the fullest as anyone can live. God gave me the title to this book because I feel each of us can be a *rose of thanks*. God gave me each verse to each poem in this book. I'm glad He did, because I love to write for the Lord.

My desire is that all that read my book will be inspired to share this book with someone else. The words to my poems were crafted with inspiration, dedication and my love for God.

Everyone has a story to tell and everyone is a poem. May you, the reader, be blessed as you read the poetical expressions in my book. May they serve a purpose in your life as they serve a purpose in mine.

There was someone all along the way that encouraged me to never give up on writing. Many times I did want to give up on writing. I became distracted, but God always brought me back to my love of writing for him.

May peace be with you and love, and may you be that *rose of thanks* that God wants all of us to be.

Myrtle F. Jackson---

ACKNOWLEDGMENTS

I have been truly blessed in my literary endeavors, and there are some people I would like to thank.

First, to God and Jesus Christ, our Savior—without Him, the writing of this book would not have been possible. Every time a door closed, God opened another one, and I give Him all of the glory and all of the praise.

Where would I be without the men in my life? To my husband, Ray, and my two sons, Richard and Justin; you are very special to me. Thank you for being my audience and for telling me what sounded good and what didn't. When I didn't want to write, you inspired me to never quit. You are wonderful, and I love you.

To my sister, Freddie who listened to my poems and told me what sounded good and what didn't. To my friends who inspired me with writing; Annie Jackson, Dian Sims, Carol Connor, Sheila Simons, Olene Bergeron, Lula Hawkins, Djuna Scott, Erna Berry, Georgia Meeks, Linda Moore, Wanza Guyton, Claudia Joplin, Barbara Baylor, Lisa Alexander, Delores Guillory and Janice Fuller.

To my pastor and his wife, the Reverend M. C. Walker Sr. and Sharon K. Walker, and the entire East Nineteenth Street Baptist Church family: I might as well say I got my start at the East Nineteenth Street Baptist Church. Thank you for praying for me. Don't stop now. (Smile.) I thank you for having confidence in me to speak poetically at so many programs.

Also thanks to the Writers' League of Texas for accepting me as a member and for being such a resourceful and educational tool.

I thank family and all of the readers who have purchased my books, passed the word on, and continued to show me love and support. As a poet, I am nothing without God and you, the audience.

Until the next book... enjoy, and thanks for the love.

A Birthday Prayer

I have a birthday prayer;
It is meant for you.
I pray that God will bless you
In everything you do.
May your days be very happy
And put a smile on your face.
May each joyous moment
Be filled with God's embrace.
Until your birthday comes again,
This is my birthday prayer.
It's filled with lots of love,
With cheerful thoughts and care!

A Birthday Wish

Without a birthday wish,
What would a birthday be?
No candles to blow out
Or fun for birthday glee!
So here's a birthday wish.
It means a lot to say
You're wished joy always,
Especially today!

Myrtle F. Jackson

A Birthday Wish for Someone Nice

You are always nice,
Caring and thoughtful too.
I hope your birthday is blessed
Today and all year through.
And hopefully your niceness
Will spread along the way.
With love, peace, and happiness,
You're wished this special day.

A Father's ABCs

Always aware
    Bills to pay
Commitment in his heart
    Devoted his way
Experience achieved
    Family he will protect
Gratitude always
    Home he won't neglect
Involved with his children
    Jesus he will obey
Knowledge he's attained
    Loves every day
Motivation in him
    Now is the key
Objectively focused
    Provider he will be
Quick to understand
    Rejoices in the Lord
Strong with strength
    Trusts in God
Useful he feels
    Vision has he
Witness for God
    X-ceedingly
Yesteryear's past
    Zestful is he.

Myrtle F. Jackson

All That Matters

It doesn't matter if you're rich
Or glorified with fame,
Or how many people love you
Or really know your name.
It doesn't matter if you're white,
Black, yellow, or brown,
Or if you're always smiling
Or sometimes wearing a frown.
It doesn't matter when you die
What people will dare to say;
The work that you've accomplished
Will speak volumes anyway.
All that really matters
Is if you've been born again,
And surely if you have
Eternally you'll win.

Almighty Lord and King

There is a higher being;
His name is Jehovah God.
He oversees the universe
In the highest regard.
His awesome power is comforting
In everything He does.
He has extreme vision
And caresses us with love.
He gives to every heart
That receives His holy ways,
A spirit, a renewed soul
For the rest of their days.
He reaches out to unbelievers
Who reject Him with sin
He gives them the chance
To come to Him and win.
Our God is very faithful;
His praise forever rings.
He gave us Christ, our Savior,
Almighty Lord and King.

A Real True Friend

I have cried upon your shoulder
And confided in you too.
     You have listened to my problems
In whatever you seem to do.
     If I have a secret
I can tell you and then
     My heart will be at ease
'Cause you are that kind of friend.
     I know that you are trustworthy;
You've shared my ups and downs.
     You are a real true friend
And fun to be around.
     And if I had to choose a friend,
My choice would surely be few
     'Cause there is no other friend
Who is as dear and sweet as you!

Awesome Power

Pink petals of serenity
Around a bar of blue
Wrapped with pure unity
For each of us anew.
Crafted in a beauty seal
That's stamped from God above,
Everything with its text
Is approved by His love.
Guided by His awesome power,
Little fish swim in the stream.
A fresh fragrance in the air
Is gentle and serene.
God is the higher power
That reaches to the shore,
And life beneath His wings
Dwells within and more.

Beautiful Songs of God

Beautiful songs of God
Fill my cup each day.
    Look where the Lord has brought us;
Lift Him up, I say.
    I am leaning on an everlasting arm
Because Jesus paid it all,
    And there is blessed assurance
That His name I will call.
    I am on the battlefield
With this little light of mine.
    There will be no turning back;
My little light will shine.
    We must take one day at a time—
Please, God, order my steps.
    What a friend we have in Jesus;
Our souls in Him are kept.
    Just a little talk with Jesus
And a closer walk with Thee,
    We serve a mighty Savior
Oh so heavenly!
    Amazing grace, I will trust in Him.
Whom shall I fear?
    Take my hand, precious Lord,
And whisper in my ear.
    Yes, Jesus loves me
In each and every way.
    I know that He lives
In my heart today.

God calms and soothes our souls
When He says, "Peace be still."
We forever believe in Him
Because God is real.
Beautiful songs of God
Praise His holy name.
I am so grateful Oh King;
I won't complain.

Blessings

Take each blessing seriously
For it may not come again.
Our God up in heaven
His love He will send.
He will bless us with prosperity
As well as with strength.
Whatever we ask of Him,
His promise will be sent.
He manifests within our thoughts
In sight of godly lessons
For us to receive and use
From His wonderful blessings!

Bread of Life

"I am the bread of life,"
The voice of God declares.
    His faithfulness instills
In each of us aware.
    If we are in the dark,
And we fall or stumble,
    Trust in God evermore
For He will keep us humble.
    His love has no limits;
It's boundless and transcends
    Peace and joy forever.
Is sacred to the end.

Myrtle F. Jackson

Built with His Hands

Early in the morn
The sun begins to rise;
   It peeps out from a hill
Deep in the sky.
   The breath of morning ushers
In a new day of birth.
   Sweetness fills the air
Here upon the earth.
   Late in the evening
The sun takes its place,
   Hiding behind a hill
From view of every face.
   The night welcomes in
The great evening stars,
   Sparkling in the sky
From near and afar.
   Forever God is present;
He controls the earth
   And everything inside
The world since its birth.
   Built with His vision,
God had a plan.
   All of creation was
Built with His hands.

Christ Is the Reason

Christ, our Savior,
From heaven above
    Reigns over the earth
In heavenly love.
    He stayed in a manger
For all to see;
    Mary and Joseph
Accepting Thee.
    So, to all
This special season,
    Celebrate Christmas.
Christ is the reason.

Myrtle F. Jackson

Church

A church is built with hands,
Wisdom, and understanding,
    For service in the sanctuary
As the Lord commanded.
    According to His word,
His work will never falter.
    We pray for one another
Gathered at the altar.
    The church is sanctified
With sweet recognition.
    In conclusion of the service
There is holy benediction.

Close to Thee

When your heart is saddened
And you feel so all alone,
Remember God, our Father,
Sits above on His throne.
He will be the only one
Who can dry your weeping eyes,
Comfort you, and strengthen you
Each time you seem to cry.
No matter how gloomy
Your days may seem to be,
Trust our heavenly Father;
He'll keep you close to Thee.

Myrtle F. Jackson

Cradle

When we are born into this world,
God invites us in.
    We come in with a clean slate
And free from any sin.
    Beginning at the cradle,
God holds the key;
    He unlocks the door
To the future for us to see.
    It is up to us,
Our souls to be saved.
    God breathes upon us
From the cradle to the grave.

Don't Let the Devil Fool You

Don't let the devil fool you—
He is evil and he's slick.
    He will corrupt your life,
And he'll do it really quick.
    You won't recognize him;
He will appear in many ways,
    With devilish smiles and handshakes
To confuse your sunny days.
    He will walk into your life
Tearing it apart.
    Enjoying every moment
Because he doesn't have a heart.
    Don't let the devil fool you—
He can also be a "she,"
    With a fancy walk and talk
And as sexy as can be.
    Yes, in this old life, remember
In whatever you decide to do,
    Hold on to Christ, our Savior.
Don't let the devil fool you.

Don't Wait

Don't wait another minute
Second, hour, or day
To forgive someone who has hurt you
All along the way.
Do whatever you can
And don't ask why.
Every minute counts
As it passes by.
When we forgive others,
God forgives us too.
He wants to instill
Courage within you.
Don't wait another hour
To visit the ill
Because when you visit,
You're doing God's will.
Don't wait another day
To put off a task;
Continuing to put it off
May be your last.
Whatever you do
Here's advice to take:
Do it now
And don't wait.

Each

Each drop of rain
That falls from the sky,
God is saying,
"The earth is dry."
Each new leaf
That buds from a tree,
God is saying,
"Enjoy and see."
Each new flower
That blooms every spring
Is such a delight
Of what God will bring.
God is close,
Within our reach.
Everyone is special
And special is *each*.

Easter

E is for eternal,
Christ's love is forever.
A is for adorable,
He'll never leave us, ever.
S is for salvation,
He gave it to us free.
T is for trust,
He paid a debt for you and me.
E is for Easter,
Such a holy day.
R is for risen,
Where Christ died and laid.

Ever True

Listen if you want to hear
A word from on high
Whispered in your ear;
Be still, God is nigh.
You will feel secure
And never be alone.
Jesus will embrace you
Above from His throne.
When your heart feels empty
And peace won't be still,
You can rest assured
God's promise will fulfill.
Everything He said
He surely will do.
Be forever mindful
His work is ever true.

Myrtle F. Jackson

Evident and Clear

God is a counselor,
A provider from above.
He guides and directs us
With His most holy love.
He is forever faithful,
Patient and sincere,
Joyful and heartfelt.
Evident and clear.
His works are marvelous,
Wondrous far and near.
The word of God is righteous
And evident and clear.

Family Feuds

Families and in-laws
Racking their brains,
Causing confusion
With hurt and pain.
It's called "family feuds,"
An unhappy name.
Everyone's changed;
No one's the same.
Hating and lying,
Deceit and more,
Untrustworthy and cruelty
Makes one sore.
Well, this is for real,
And it's bad news:
There are no blessings
In family feuds!

Foreign Place

Across the land and sea,
Iraq's a foreign place.
So many dying in this country
At such a rapid pace.
Out on the battlefield
US soldier's tears
Are filled with hurt and pain.
This war is really real.
US soldiers dying
And those who remain
Really are protecting us
Across our country's plains.
For many years to come,
We will need amazing grace
From God who is sovereign
In this foreign place.

Forever Near

Beneath the realm of beauty
Lies an ugly mess
Because old evil Satan
Wants to put us to the test.
God will test us too;
Forever God will win.
The mighty hand of God
Overpowers any sin.
Be careful of old Satan—
He will test you every day.
If you're not close to God,
Satan will have his way.
God will defend us;
To Him we are dear.
All we need is trust.
He is forever near.

Myrtle F. Jackson

God Embraces Us with Faith

Clouds soar beneath the heavens,
Gloomy upon the earth.
Our Father above the clouds
Begins His heavenly search.
He gives His command,
Guiding the turbulent storms.
Fear is removed from us
As He wraps us in His arms.
If thoughts are insecure,
God almighty waits.
He dismisses any doubt
And embraces us with faith.

God in Disguise

I visited a church one Sunday;
The church was filled with love.
Everyone was celebrating
And praising God above.
Church was exciting;
It is where one belongs.
Everyone was clapping
And singing great songs.
There entered a man
Who sat quietly in a pew.
No one noticed him;
He seemed really blue.
He began enjoying
The great gospel hymns.
The choir voices elevated,
Each song seemed for him.
Oh, the songs of Zion,
They echoed so high.
This poor lonesome man
Then began to sigh.
The songs so touched him
That he rose to his feet.
He began to clap and shout,
"This music sounds so sweet."
Tears flowed down his face,
His heart ached inside,
For the people did not notice
He too was God's child.

Somehow he touched everyone;
He had a special glee.
One had to be born again
To really look and see
A light within his heart
Shined through his soul.
His love was immeasurable,
Impossible to unfold.
He received with his heart
The Father, Holy Ghost, and Son.
He was born again
And joy he had won.
Indeed, be very careful
And be very wise.
The one we ignore
May be God in disguise.

Grace

There is no substitute
For our beloved God.
If we become destitute,
We can call on our Lord.
Without God's grace
We become very scared,
Weak, troubled, and timid
With challenges to bear.
God's light shines
From the paradise land.
It shines bright and fine
For all of man.
God's grace protects us
When we're in a storm.
Forever we can trust Him
And cling to His arms.
Our God is supreme.
Oh, bless the human race
With never-ending love
And everlasting grace.

God's Love

God's love is gentle,
Kind, faithful, and true,
Patient and forgiving
And magnificent too.
His love is everlasting,
Dear, sweet, and bold,
Adorable and more precious
Than silver or gold.
His love is gracious,
Beautiful, and great,
Peaceful and soft
When we meditate.
God's love is strong
And comforts us inside.
He is encouragement
Where confidence abides.
God's love is calm,
Soothing from above.
Nothing is more nurturing
Than God's love.

Guide Us

Guide us, heavenly dove,
Remove what is dark.
As we capture your love,
Your will we embark.
Wash us, heavenly Father,
Let Thy light shine
With joy eternally.
Thy holy will is thine.
Guide us with protection
Along harm's way;
Hold on to us firmly
Each and every day.
In You there is strength,
Love, peace, and trust.
With devotion so divine,
Please guide us.

Myrtle F. Jackson

He Is Enough

When fleeing from temptation,
It can be rough.
We must not forget
God is enough.
Witnessing to our brethren
Truly is a must.
No idols, please,
'Cause He is enough.
All who believe
Sincerely trust
God's eternal greatness!
He is enough.

He Really Cares

You don't have to worry
When God is by your side.
He knows when you're hurting;
In Him you can confide.
Whenever you are lonely,
God is surely there.
He loves and comforts you.
I know He really cares.
And just because He cares,
You are safe and strong.
God watches over you
As He sits on the throne.

He Will Embrace you with His Love

When sadness overcomes you
And your heart is heavy too,
    God will lift your heavy heart
From deep inside of you.
    Remember that your loved one
Is gone for a while.
    Cherish the memories
That made you laugh and smile.
    One day you will be reunited,
Standing in heaven's way.
    You will see your loved one again
On that great and faithful day.
    Until that day arrives,
God watches from above.
    He will secure your every need;
He will embrace you with His love.

He Will Fix
What is Wrong

If I could dry your tears,
I'd make them go away.
    You'd never cry again
Forever and a day.
    If I could look inside
Your aching, broken heart,
    I would carefully mend it
For a new, happy start.
    If I could see you smile
With joy on your face,
    You would make the world better
And such a happy place.
    If I could take your troubles
And put them in my care,
    They all would disappear
You would have none to bear.
    But since I cannot,
I am weak; God is strong.
    Call on His name.
He will fix what is wrong.

His Blood Made Us Free

They nailed Him to the cross,
His arms stretched wide,
    With nails in His hands
And blood on His side.
    Did Jesus die for you?
Did He die for me?
    Yes, He did, indeed He did.
His blood made us free.
    And because of His blood,
There is no fear.
    Jesus lives forever.
He is right here.

His Promise Unfolds

The moon appears
Hallowed by night,
    Renewed from darkness
And into light.
    Oh, glorious gift,
Thy shining star
    Glows up above
From heaven afar.
    The presence of God
Glimmers in our souls.
    The love for us
His promise unfolds.
    As it unfolds
His word instills
    Obedience in us
To do His will.
    God promises above
He will never leave
    Us all alone
'Cause we believe.
    Though we are aware
God shapes and molds,
    We know for sure
His promise unfolds.

Myrtle F. Jackson

Holy Easter Morn

Holy, wonderful Jesus
Hidden behind a tomb,
    There He lay motionless
But would rise soon!
    The world would be amazed
To know Jesus lives.
    He died and He rose
To heal and forgive.
    Why, Savior, why
Were thorns embedded in
    Atop Thy head?
Just to wash away our sins?
    Holy, precious Jesus,
Praise God you were born.
    Jesus died and rose
On holy Easter morn.

Honest Working Jobs

If you see a man
With crack in his hand,
    Get away from him
As fast as you can.
    He could rob your mind
If you're within his reach.
    He will pull you down
Like an animal in the street.
    An honest working job
Is to make an honest living.
    Flee from crime and drugs,
And you won't feel driven.
    Honest work is honored
In the presence of God.
    Whether you're a waiter
Or mowing someone's lawn,
    Whether you're a clerk
In a mail room
    Or a schoolteacher
In a classroom,
    Whether you're a painter
Or a cashier at a store
    Or a sales associate
Selling merchandise galore,
    Whether you're a chef
Or washing dirty dishes
    Or collecting trash
On trash trucks and hitches,
    They are honest work
If it is pleasing to God.
    God loves honest people
With honest working jobs!

Myrtle F. Jackson

Humble Yourself to Jesus

We must humble ourselves to Jesus
When we have sinned,
   Confess ungodly habits.
Our hearts He will cleanse
   Jesus Christ is merciful,
His works sweet to taste.
   When we humble ourselves to Him,
He saves us with grace.
   God will not destroy us;
Instead He will bless
   Each heart collectively
As our sins we confess.
   A thankful heart is soothing
Because no one else
   Can instill peace and joy
Like God in ourselves.

I Am

I am the one
Who shines the light;
I am the one
Who draws the night.
I am the one
Who creates the day,
With stream-filled scenes
Across the bay.
I am the one
You cannot see
Who controls the wind,
Flowers, and trees.
I am the one
Who breathes the dew
On morning grass,
Fresh and renewed.
I am the one
Who make birds fly,
Controls the earth
And heavenly sky.
I am the one
Who feeds the land
With nourishing food
From my hand.
I am the one
Who controls the birth
Of human souls
Upon this earth.

Myrtle F. Jackson

I am the one
Who controls death,
    The beginning and end
Of each life's breath.
    I am the one,
O' holy lamb,
    Who gave you Christ!
God I am!

If I Could Count All of My Blessings

If I could count all of my blessings,
I wouldn't know where to start.
   I guess I'd start with health and strength
And a happy, happy heart.
   I'd count the many times
God has heard my plea.
   When I was weak and frightened,
He came to rescue me.
   I'd count the many days
With tears in my eyes.
   God wiped them all away;
I never asked Him why.
   I'd count the many times
God fed me with His hand.
   If there was any doubt,
He'd make me understand.
   I'd count every minute
He gave me air to breathe,
   And I'd count each new day
He blessed me with to see.
   Though I can't count all of the blessings
I have received from above,
   I surely can count each day
I am blessed with His love.

Myrtle F. Jackson

If I Fall

If I fall
Do not laugh,
   For my stumbling
Soon will pass.
   Instead of laughing,
Pick me up
   And pray for me.
Lord, fill my cup
   With Thy love
From heaven's grace.
   Use me, Lord,
In this place.
   If I fall
Do not sigh
   Or even ask
The question "why."
   If I fall
Do not say
   Negative words
That hurt each day.
   Just be kind
I ask of all.
   I'll get up
If I fall.

I'm Glad You're a Friend

When I think of you,
A smile brush my face,
Of happy caring moments
All filled with loving grace.
You're always so kind,
Loving and gentle too,
And graciously grateful
In everything you do!
I'm glad to have a friend
Enlightened with Christian love,
An everlasting friendship
That's blessed from above.

I Missed Your Birthday

I'm sorry I missed your birthday.
It really slipped my mind.
    I hope you had a happy one,
A joyous and blessed time.

Inhale the Future, Exhale the Past!

Inhale the blessings
Received from our God;
   Exhale the rugged path
On the road where we trod.
   Inhale the goodness
Abundant behind God's door;
   Exhale the badness,
Unfortunates and more.
   Inhale the future—
God is always true;
   Exhale the past—
He will redeem you.

Myrtle F. Jackson

In Him You Are Secure

The greatest peace is knowing
When others share your grief,
And the greatest strength of all
Is in your own belief.
When you believe in God,
He will keep you near,
Comfort and strengthen you
And hold you so dear.
And because God is near,
You can rest assured
God will not forsake you;
In Him you are secure.

Inside His Holy Power

When our thoughts assemble
They purposely proceed.
    The holy righteous spirit
In everything we need
    United in the evening,
Human touch we grasp
    Of sighted vision awareness
With mindless to relapse
    Abound by heavenly glory,
Elevation high,
    Told of faithful story
Thy great throne is nigh.
    And because of reflection
In days to pass
    Of minutes and hours
In spiritual mass,
    No questions but answers
Within this holy hour
    Of God's acclamation
Inside His holy power.

Myrtle F. Jackson

Jesus

When we call the name of Jesus,
Our Savior will hear,
Whether our cry is far away
Or whether our cry is near.
There is a profound inner peace
Christ gives us to belong.
It doesn't matter the circumstance;
His strength will make us strong.
When we call the name of Jesus,
He will surely come to us
And wrap His arms around our hearts.
In Jesus's name we trust.

Joy

Joy is a heavenly gift
That manifests within,
   Peace and holiness
And beauty that transcends.
   Deep down in our hearts,
God makes us whole,
   Blessing us with a light
That shines bright and bold.
   As we journey all abroad
A long way from home,
   God instills joy faithfully
Wherever we may roam.

Myrtle F. Jackson

Kindness Is Contagious

Kindness is contagious;
It can spread anywhere,
When we give a smile or two
To show someone we care.
There may be others
We may have missed.
When kindness is multiplied,
We have a kindness list.
The kindness list includes
Selfish days are gone,
Sharing with others,
Making them feel at home,
Calling up someone
Who lives far away
Just to let her know
You thought of them that day.
Kindness is contagious;
Please don't let it stop.
When kindness is multiplied,
Kindness really rocks!

Life Is Like a Vapor

Life is like a vapor.
The mist disappears
Like minutes in an hour
And months in a year,
Like steam from the earth
And dew mist from the grass.
Life is like a vapor.
How swiftly time passes.

Myrtle F. Jackson

Life's Test

When God sends His angel,
We really have to go
    Whether we are prepared or not.
God loves us so.
    His angel will lead us;
God will take our hand.
    We will leave many behind,
But they all will understand.
    God welcomes His saints
With open arms and rest.
    He will open the book
To the life's test.
    Surely when we've passed,
On earth there will be a void.
    In heaven there is peace
When we're safe with the Lord.

Love

When we fall in love,
Our hearts skip a beat
Of that special someone
Who will make our lives complete.
Falling in love is wonderful
When both of you confess
The love both are feeling;
You two are really blessed.
United in holy matrimony
And sealed with a kiss,
Your union is really special
With God's heavenly bliss.

Love in Valentines

What is in a valentine
For you and for me?
Is it wrapped in love from God
For every heart to see?
Yes, it is in every way,
And every loving face
Will see much love and sunshine
In such a loving place.
Feel the love in valentines,
Caress it with your heart.
God will caress it too
Before love even starts.

Meditation

There is peace in meditation
When we submit ourselves
To Jesus Christ, our Savior,
And to no one else.
In true submission,
With sincere dedication,
Our thoughts are energized
In holy meditation.
Our Holy Father's lordship,
His great expectations,
Remain faithful
In prayer and meditation.

Myrtle F. Jackson

Mother

Everything about a mother
Is as sweet as can be.
Mother is your friend
And always trustworthy.
Mother is a warrior;
She does not cease in prayer.
She teaches and trains her children.
A mother really cares.
Sometimes a mother
Is mother and daddy too.
She has tasks and challenges,
But she still takes care of you.
Mother lends support
No matter where you are.
She'll lift you up and cheer you on;
Her presence is never far.
Who can be so kind
And loving like no other?
No one but a gift from God:
We call her "Mother."

Mother Is Special

Mother is special.
She does things a mother does,
    Like wash your clothes and cook your food
And give you lots of love.
    She listens to your problems
And solves them if she can,
    Disciplines you accordingly,
She has a daily plan.
    She pays the bills and grocery shops
At the community store.
    She helps you with your homework
And does so much more.
    Once you are all grown up
And out on your own,
    A mother's love is always with you
When you're away from home.
    Mother is special;
No other can take her place.
    Her heart is always with you—
And her smiling face.

Myrtle F. Jackson

No More

There is a heavenly door;
Behind it God abides.
When this life is over,
We all can go inside.
No more cussing and fussing,
No more cheating and lying,
No more hurting others,
No more pain and dying.
No more jealousy and hate,
No more hot and cold,
No more famine in the land,
No more sinning souls.
No more diabetes and cancer
Tearing our bodies apart,
No more pills to take
When we're with the Lord.
Only peace and happiness
Is behind heaven's door,
And if Satan tries to enter,
God will say, "No more."

Oh, What a Beautiful Day

Oh, what a beautiful day,
Prose and poetry in May.
  Writing makes one's day.
Oh, what a beautiful day.
  Oh, what a beautiful night,
Stars in the sky shine bright.
  They glow in the evening light.
Oh, what a beautiful night.
  Oh, what beautiful land,
Made for all of man
  By God's almighty hand.
Oh, what beautiful land.
  Oh, what a beautiful moon,
Most beautiful on a night in June
  When one is singing a tune.
Under such a beautiful moon.
  Oh, what a beautiful day,
The wind blowing one's way
  And the clouds no longer gray.
Oh, what a beautiful day.

Our Hearts He Will Mend

We cannot solve a problem
Without knowing what it is.
Jesus can solve any problem
Because fixing it is His.
And when Jesus fixes it,
The problem disappears
For our Savior can mend
Broken hearts and tears.
He produces sureness
And compassionate devotion
And mends together
Our every emotion.
Our God is faithful
No other can we depend.
When there are disappointments,
Our hearts He will mend.

Our Life Seems Brighter

Our Almighty God
Knows when we are stressed;
    He gently calms and soothes us
When we've made a mess.
    Our lives seem brighter.
A different view to Thee,
    When we acknowledge His goodness.
He dwells in you and me.
    It doesn't matter where we are
Or where we decide to go;
    If we are lost, he will find us.
No other one I know.
    And all of the heavy burdens
Begin to get much lighter.
    When God is in our hearts,
Our life seems brighter.

Myrtle F. Jackson

Our Love Is Real

Our love is real
Today and forever.
God is in our lives
As we unite together.
Our marriage is special
Right here and right now.
We will truly honor
Our sacred marriage vows.
This is our new beginning;
This is our new life.
We will cherish our love
As husband and wife.
We are now one heartbeat
That beats instead.
We will always remember
This special day we wed.
Our love is real
Today and forever.
God, please bless this union
As we join together.

Peace

One should feel calm
When peace invades the heart.
It draws a spiritual web
Just like a piece of art.
It renews and nurtures
All day long.
It comforts and empowers.
No, you're not alone.
This thing call peace
Centers inside the soul.
It unravels the inner fears
That surfaced long ago.
It quiets the soulfulness,
And the quiet will never cease
For it surrounds every angle
Of this gifted act called peace.

Penny

God and I have a secret;
He lets me know He's near.
    I can always feel His presence
'Cause a penny will appear.
    It is always just one penny,
Never two or never three.
    It appears in unique places;
No one can see it but me.
    Sometimes I will find a penny
Hidden alone on the floor;
    Sometimes there's one on a counter
Or one visible beneath a door.
    It is not my imagination;
It is not just a dream.
    God can transform Himself
Into the most precious little things.
    These pennies are not lost
By family, friend, or foe.
    They are uniquely planted
Everywhere I go.
    My little secret with God
Is undiscovered by many.
    Only the anointed can see Him
In the shape of a penny.

People Who Are Mean

Mean people are hateful.
They have corrupted ways
And toxic communication
With ugly words to say.
They will smile in your face
But stab you in the back,
Pretend that they like you
To keep you off track.
They will begin to dig a hole
Just for little ol' you,
But what they don't know is
They'd better dig two.
Mean people attack anyone;
Their hearts are unclean.
We know God will deal with
People who are mean.

Myrtle F. Jackson

Poet's Inspiration

I pray each time I write
For guidance from above.
I pray that my thoughts
Are blessed with God's love.
God gives me inspiration
That I add in every verse.
My words are directed
Embraced with His worth
My words are filled
With deep meditation.
Look into my heart and see
A poet's inspiration.

A Poet's Vision

Creativity is a poet,
An authentic one with ease—
Poetry in motion,
Words that make me free.
Happy and collective
With life's mechanical woo(s),
Joyful moments of contentment
And not the weary blues.
A poet's real vision
Is for the world to see.
Poetical expressions
Are possibilities.

Pray a Daily Prayer

If you are laden
With discontent, despair,
    Doubt, fear, or anger,
Pray a daily prayer.
    If you are restless
On a path of uncare,
    With overwhelming circumstances,
Pray a daily prayer.
    Every stumbling block
Always seem unfair.
    If encouragement is gone,
Pray a daily prayer,
    For Jesus Christ, our Savior,
The cross He did bear.
    Trust in Jesus always;
Pray a daily prayer.

Qualified Is Jesus

    Qualified is Jesus,
He is the best
    With experience in everything,
We all can attest.
    We trust Him because He's love,
He is peace, and He is sure
    To save the soul of anyone
Who wants their life secure.
    Jesus loves us all;
No one is denied.
    Christ lives forever
Because He's qualified.

Remembering Mother

Who can repay mother
For the love she has shown?
She cares for her children
Until they are grown.
Her love doesn't end there,
Whether she's gone or she's here.
Her children are in her heart;
She holds them very dear.
When children grow up,
They will surely see
How mother taught them
To be all they can be.
Honor your mother on Mother's Day.
She is irreplaceable like no other.
God will bless you
For remembering Mother.

Right Now Today

Whatever your will,
Whatever you say,
   Strengthen us, Lord,
Right now today.
   Lift our hearts;
Don't let us stray.
   We need Thee now,
Right now today.
   Watch over us, Lord,
Where we lie
   Keep us safe
Right now today.
   And after we've done
It all your way,
   Bless us, Lord,
Right now today.

Myrtle F. Jackson

Say Thank You,
Say I'm Sorry

If I didn't say thank you,
I really didn't forget.
I'm adding them all up
To say with the rest.
If I didn't say I'm sorry,
It's really not meant to be;
To overlook your feelings
Is not a part of me.
When I say thank you,
I appreciate you,
And when I say I'm sorry
I mean it. It's true!

A Small Surprise

A small surprise is not shoes
Or clothing from a store.
It is not fancy jewelry
Or perfume la 'more.
It is not a fancy hat
We wear on our head.
It is not satin sheets
To beautify a bed.
It is when you get a call
From a long-lost friend.
That moment is cherished
From that day till the end.
It is when you see someone
You haven't seen for a while,
And inside your heart
Is a great big smile.
It is when your enemy
Asks, "Will you please forgive me?"
You never thought you'd say yes,
But it made your heart free.
So God can transform Himself—
Because He's very wise—
And use you and me
As a small surprise.

Myrtle F. Jackson

Sinner

Sinner, unholy, with sinful ways,
Bow your head in prayer.
Pray, repent for righteous days;
Our savior really cares.
He wants to save your soul
From sin and disgust.
Your hand He will hold
If only you will trust.
You can be saved
And become a winner.
Rejoice in overcoming
From being a sinner.

Soft, Gentle Touch

Sometimes when in doubt,
If you need a crutch,
Lean on Christ, our Savior,
He loves you very much.
He will touch you gently,
So please be aware
Of His holy presence.
I know He really cares.
And just because He cares,
We thank Him so much
For His loving kindness
And His soft, gentle touch.

So Long, Not Good-Bye

When you enter heaven's gate,
Our God up above
    Will look down below
And release Thy heavenly dove.
    You will be remembered
As you journey abroad,
    Serving our Savior faithfully
And kept by the Lord.
    Until that great judgment day
In God's big sky,
    We will see you again.
So long, not good-bye.

Sometimes We Like to Ponder

Sometimes we like to ponder
Jesus's love and more,
The pain that He suffered
And the heavy cross He bore.
He did it for all of us.
What more could He give
Than His holy precious life?
He wanted us to live.
Christ is so wonderful.
We never have to wonder
Of His faithfulness.
That's why we like to ponder.

Stay in School

You have worked hard
And studied in school;
You have done your homework
And passed tests too.
You have been patient
With challenging days,
And you have demonstrated
Your achievable grades.
But it does not stop now,
So you must have a vision
To continue your dreams
On this long, long mission.
You must be prepared
To attain all knowledge.
Now that you've graduated,
It is good to enter college.
From there you will journey
Down the pathway to success
Because you know
You have done your best.
In doing your best,
There is no guessing.
You have succeeded;
Consider it a blessing.
You will experience
The golden rule.
You did it! You made it!
You stayed in school.

Strength to Be Strong

Weakness can overcome us,
Make us limp and frail,
Leave us defenseless;
Our hearts too will ail.
We can call on God—
He supplies new strength,
Comfort, peace, and joy.
Inspired, we quench.
We are no longer weak;
We know where we belong
Our Father manifests
Strength to make us strong.

Surrender All of Your Burdens

Surrender all of your burdens,
No more worries for you.
God secures each burden
And embraces you too.
With peace and assurance,
Your prayers are heard.
God gently answers them
With a divine word.
Surrender all of your burdens;
It is all right.
Expressing yourself to God
Is such a delight.
An intimate relationship
With God you will win;
His arms are open wide
And trust he extends.

Sweet Recognition

There is sweet recognition
In each appointed life,
When gifts from God are used
In the name of Jesus Christ.
And when we use these gifts
Our talents are delight
It pleases God forevermore
And magnifies our sight
To pray for one another
In sweet benediction.
Then God will reward us
With sweet recognition.

Myrtle F. Jackson

Teatime with Christ

Hot tea or cold tea,
It is all right
To have a godly party:
Teatime with Christ.
Tea presents wisdom;
It's a wonderful zeal.
It flows down the throat
Like a river so real.
The first sip of tea
Always tastes the best.
We stir the art of life
And then drink the rest.
And after a cup of tea,
We have a clear eye
To spread our thoughts
Like a bird in the sky.
We wear dressy attire
And chat a little while
Over this fragranced liquid
That makes us smile.
Teatime with Christ
Is happily bold.
When we drink tea slowly,
It relaxes the soul.
It lubricates the mind,
And moistens the lips.
There is so much beauty
In every tea sip.
Be eloquent and sweet
In your inspiring life.
Take time out often
To have tea with Christ.

Telephone Call

When dreams are shattered
And the world seems small,
    Call up God.
Make the telephone call.
    Call Him anytime,
Long distance and all.
    He will promptly answer
Your telephone call.
    You will not be put on hold,
No "one moment please,"
    No asking you what number
Or "what city please?"
    There will be no operator
To interrupt at all.
    You can talk a long time
On the telephone call.
    There are no fees to pay,
No prices on a wall,
    No recorded voice
When you make the call.
    Take advantage of this offer—
It is free to all.
    It doesn't matter where you live;
Just make the call.

Myrtle F. Jackson

Thank God

Thank God for beauty
In the serene, splendor hour—
The freshness of a lily
And the beauty in its flower.
Thank God for the darkness
And the shining, twinkling stars
That shine so brightly
Both near and far.
Most of all thank God
For being our eyes to see.
He is the only one
Who make us free.

Thanksgiving Season

Thank our Savior
High from above.
    Amazing blessings
Along with love.
    Be kind to all,
Share indeed,
    Give to others
In desperate need.
    Victorious this season,
Inspired by God,
    Near and far
Go and trod.
    Share each blessing
Everywhere you go,
    And acknowledge God
So He will know.
    Only from Him, blessed are we
Never will He neglect us
    When we're in need.

Myrtle F. Jackson

The Foolish Ones

God forgive the foolish ones
Not listening to His word,
    Abandoning every righteousness thought,
Expressions are unheard.
    Forgive their evil eyes,
Their wicked, hateful ways,
    Uncaring minds and hearts,
And unappreciated days,
    Satan's heart is evil too.
His work is never done.
    Those who follow him
Are the foolish ones.

The Glass House

Imagine a glass house:
Happiness dwells inside.
　Next door is the ocean
Where one can watch the tides.
　Chandeliers hang in every room
With such distinguished pride.
　Furniture all in its place,
Blessings much obliged.
　The carpet is white and plush,
Free from any stains.
　All must take their shoes off
When entering from the rain.
　Flowers are assembled all around
Inside the house and out;
　Each bouquet is fresh,
Their fragrance all about.
　The grass is well maintained
And such a pretty green;
　It complements the hedges.
Oh, what a beautiful scene.
　A happy family resides here.
They are happy all the time.
　They read their Bible daily
And seem to be doing fine.
　Then all of a sudden
Tidal waves intrude,
　Washing away the glass house
And the family too.

The family struggled with the tides,
Becoming short of breath.
God rescued the family,
All escaping death.
Never again should tidal waves
Wash the family out.
God will rebuild the glass house
Solid as a rock.

The Lost Sinner

Some say a sinner
Life is full of sin,
But I say to you,
Invite Christ in.
Some say a sinner
Is a liar and a cheat,
But I say to you,
Pray for them, they're weak.
Some say a sinner
Refuses to repent,
But I say to you,
Ask God to give them strength.
Some say a sinner
Is daring and bold,
But I say to you,
Ask God to save their soul.
Some say a sinner
Just doesn't seem to care,
But I say to you,
Lift them up in prayer.
Some say a sinner
Will never be a winner,
But I say to you,
God forgives sinners.

Myrtle F. Jackson

The Promise God Made

There will be times
When you don't know what to do.
Just give it to Jesus;
He will take care of you.
He will cast your burdens
And put them in His hand.
No need to wonder,
You will understand.
When God say He loves you,
You are his very own.
He means it from His heart;
His strength will make you strong.
So when you're feeling weak,
Do not be afraid
To ask our Savior to help you
Upon the promise He has made.

The Waiting Congregation

The shepherd of God stood
And sang a holy hymn,
Praising Christ our Lord,
Faithfully worshipping Him.
People in the pew
Were the congregation.
They praised God
In holy exhortation.
The shepherd expressed,
"Repent your sins today.
Every head must bow
When you kneel to pray.
Every heart must confess
Each and every sin;
Ask for forgiveness
And invite our Savior in."
These words were embraced
With sincere exclamation,
From the shepherd of God
To the waiting congregation.

Though Clouds Are Gray

Because clouds are gray,
The day seems drear.
Raindrops fall
From far and near.
And near and far
The sun will shine,
For God will leave
The clouds behind.
Above each cloud
The sun will peep
To let us know
God is sweet.
God's hand controls
The clouds each day
To brighten us up
When clouds are gray.

Transformation of a Christian

A Christian is transformed
By the hand of God.
He molds our image
No man can ever rob.
God washes away
Dirt, grit, and grime
Until he has cleansed us
Free of any slime.
Our hearts are made whole;
Salvation we have won.
We are saved by grace—
A Christian is transformed.

Trouble Is Really Dirty

Old trouble and new trouble,
Get out of my way.
No one wants any trouble
Not now, not today.
No one likes trouble;
It will follow you around.
Sometimes trouble will sit there
And not make a sound.
Trouble has no feelings,
But it has a start and end.
It has an overloaded brain
And a heart that's cold and thin.
Trouble is not cute;
It has an ugly face.
It moves very swiftly
From place to place.
Trouble can be black,
Brown, yellow, or white.
Trouble can just trouble you
All day and all night.
Do not get into trouble
If you know what I mean.
Trouble is really dirty;
Keep your hands clean.

Try Jesus

If you've tried Jesus,
Please try Him again.
His love is sacred;
He is a good friend.
He will protect you;
He is a shield.
You can trust in Jesus;
He is really real.
When you try Jesus,
He will be right there.
No need to worry;
Christ really cares.
He is the light
That brightens the soul.
Love is instilled
Evermore to hold.

Understand

Who can understand us
When we've done a dirty deed
Or turn our back on someone
In a desperate time of need?
God will forgive us.
He always understands
How Satan is out to get us.
God rebukes Him with His hand.
Then God recaptures us,
And we become very strong.
We lean on and trust in Him
On His holy, holy throne.
Be kind and loving
Is God's command.
He is ever merciful
Because he understands.

Victorious

Anointed by God
And guaranteed His love,
He is the only one
We think highly of.
Revived by His word
So gracious and glorious,
Jesus Christ is His gift,
So righteous and victorious.
His everlasting love,
Thankfully holyous,
Is an anchor for our soul,
Wonderfully victorious.

Watchful Eye

There is someone watching us
With every walk and pace.
    His smile shines and beams
Upon every human face.
    He even watches over the mammals
And everything with wings.
    He breathes upon and embraces
The hummingbird that sings.
    He cups each flower in His hands
And shapes it from the sky.
    He sprinkles it until it grows;
Its soil is never dry.
    He calms the streams and rivers,
The oceans and the seas.
    It is God and His watchful eye
Who watches you and me.

We Didn't Come Here to Stay

The sun will rise,
The sun will set.
In the evening,
Don't you forget.
In this life,
Short or long,
Names are called
To His throne.
Live each life
In a Christian way.
It is certain
We won't stay.

Myrtle F. Jackson

When the Night
Seems Cold

When the night seems cold
And you cannot rest,
    Your thoughts unfold
Of not doing your best.
    Unravel your fears
And give them to God.
    He will lift you up.
He is a great God.
    He will take your hand
And squeeze it tight,
    Just to let you know
Everything is all right.
    When the night seems cold,
There is no limit
    Of bountiful blessings
Every second, every minute.
    God warms the heart;
He will never let us go.
    He soothes and comforts
When the night seems cold.

Without God

Without God
There could be no trees,
    No air to breathe,
No you or me.
    There would be no land,
No earth or sand,
    No human souls
Called woman or man.
    Without God
There would be no sky
    Where raindrops fall
From way up high.
    There would be no grass
With morning dew,
    No morning breath
That smells brand new.
    Without God
We would not know
    The right path to take
As we go.
    Without God
There would be no Christ
    To walk with us
In this life.
    Without God
We could not survive;
    Without God
He would not be in our lives.

Myrtle F. Jackson

Wonderful Creation

Look at God's creation.
No one can ignore.
He is marvelous,
More beautiful than before.
Without this beautification,
Earth is not the same.
That is why God is King;
We worship His holy name.
Magnificent creation,
Wonderfully divine,
All made by our Lord,
Holy God, Oh thine.

X-specially Faithful

It is not by happenstance
That God forgives our past.
We can appreciate
His love will always last.
When challenges enter our lives,
We become confused,
Senseless, and thoughtless,
And want to be amused.
But God is compassionate,
X-specially faithful.
We have assurance in our hearts;
To Him we are grateful.

Myrtle F. Jackson

You

You've got issues
Within yourself
That make you abrupt
With everyone else.
You don't care
About others' pain;
All you do
Is talk and complain.
You talk about her,
And you talk about him.
You call her "fat,"
And you call him "slim."
You really don't care
If you sin,
And when you do,
You think you'll win.
You can't be trusted,
Because you lie.
You can change,
But you just won't try.
All you do
Is talk about you,
What you've done,
And what you're going to do.
Erase your issues;
Then you will begin
A positive reflection.
You can win.

Young at Heart

Age is a number.
All of us know
    If you're young at heart,
Old you'll never grow.
    Your skin may wrinkle;
Slower your steps become.
    Your vision grows dimmer;
Strength may leave you some.
    Even if it does,
There is a brighter view.
    Always be thankful
Deep inside of you.
    Think very young
And never let go.
    It soothes your heart joyfully,
And young you'll always know.

Myrtle F. Jackson

Z-lightful

Z-lightful and sufficient
Is God's love for us.
   Our inner beings no longer wander;
In God we do trust.
   Z means God is zealous;
He is comfort and peace.
   He is inspiration;
His love will never cease.
   Z-lightfully dedicated,
God will never leave.
   He inspires us with His word
For all who believe.
   God gives all a chance
To walk a straight line
   Into the gateway of righteousness
With a holy, holy mind.

Printed in the United States
By Bookmasters